The ABCs of Chatham

Dedicated to the loves of my life:
Melissa, Marigold, and Bodie
Here's to a lifetime of Chatham memories together!

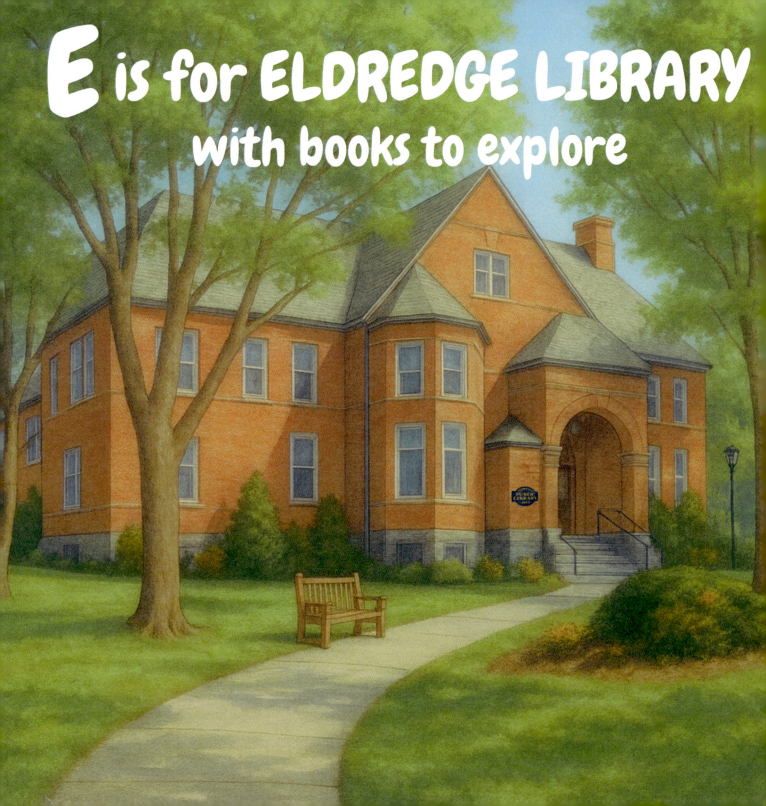

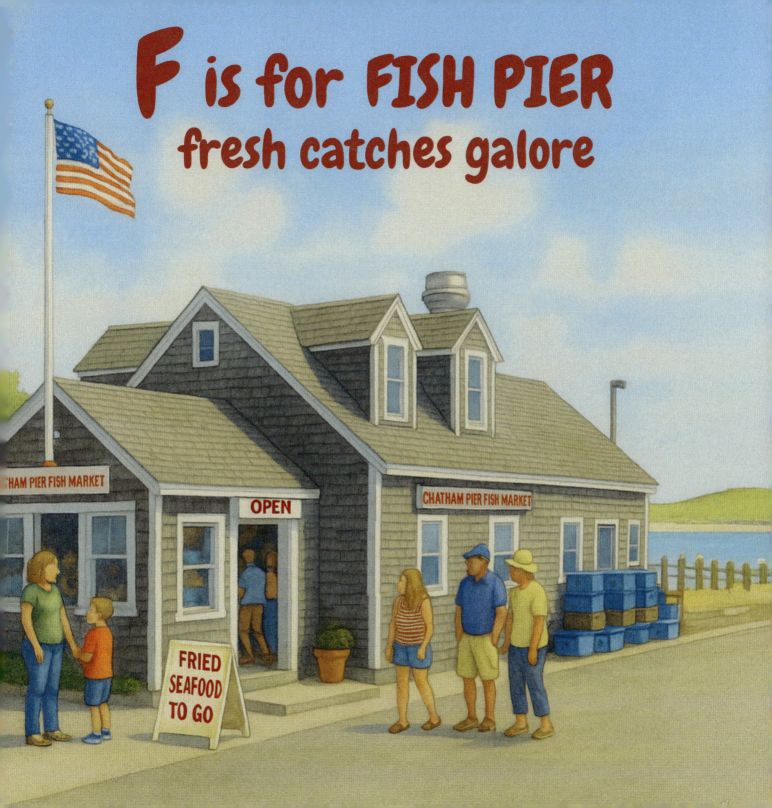

G is for GREAT WHITES
patrolling Chatham's ocean blue

H is for HARDING'S BEACH
sunset skies of every hue

I is for IMPUDENT OYSTER
with the finest of fare

M is for MONOMOY
with trails along the shore

N is for NANTUCKET SOUND
that Stage Harbor's boats explore

O is for OUTER BEACH
boats take you there

Q is for QUEEN ANNE INN
its history on display

S is for SQUIRE
with "food for the hungry, drink for the thirsty"

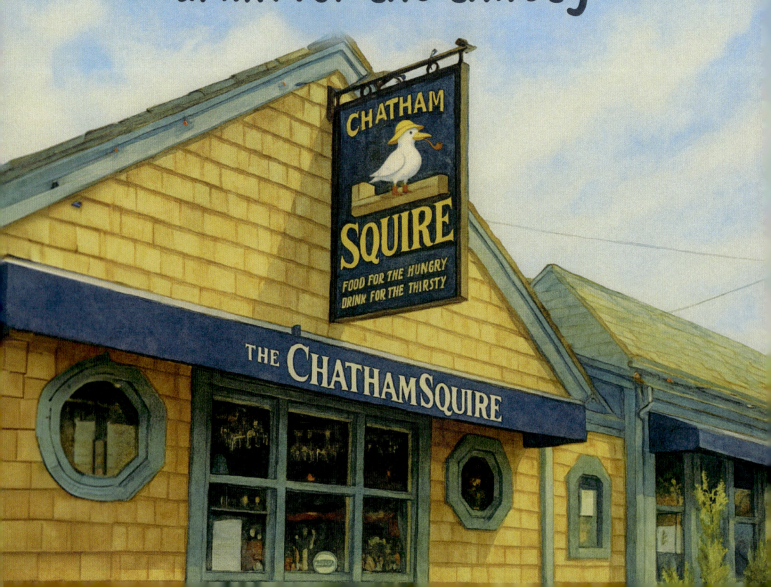

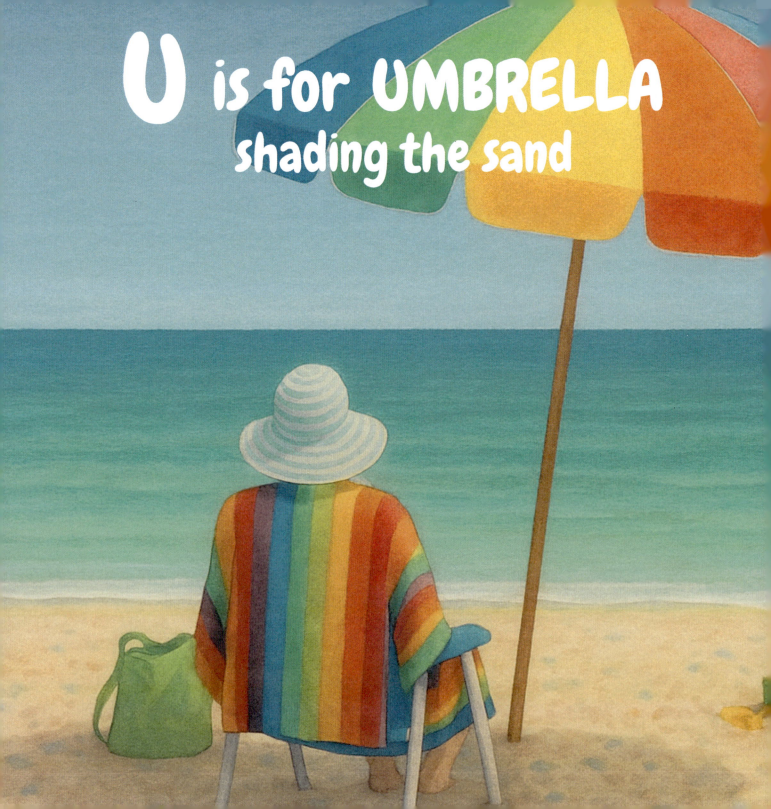

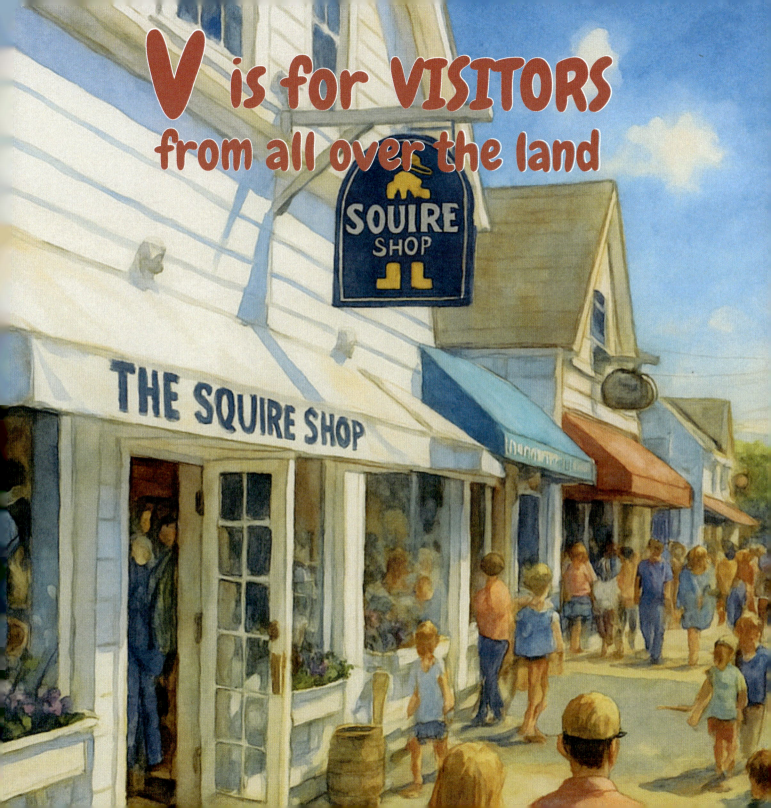

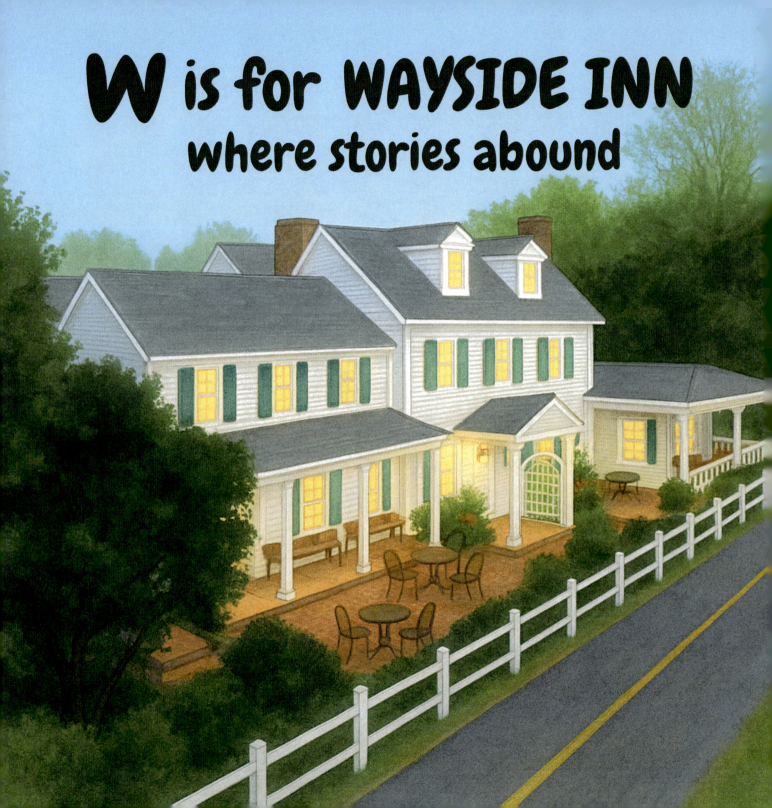

X MARKS THE SPOT
where treasure's to be found

Y is for YOGA
on Lighthouse Beach's shore

About the author:

Fitz was introduced to the magic of Chatham by his wife Melissa and her multi-generation Chatham loving family.

In 2022 Fitz and Melissa married in Chatham's St. Christopher's church, then celebrated at the Chatham Beach and Tennis Club. They have two incredible kids, Marigold and Bodie, who are the inspiration for this book.

Fitz is the Head of North America for Amazon's Design Technology team. He loves family, friends, fitness, and food. He hopes you enjoy each page of this love letter to Chatham!